AF425677

BIG Faith:

A Love Beyond Us

Irish & Trent Porter

BIG Faith: A Love Beyond Us

Copyright © 2024 by Irish Porter & Trent Porter

All rights reserved. No part of this book may be reproduced or transmitted in any form or by any means without written permission from the author.

ISBN (979-8-9898507-3-0)

MTE Publishing
mtepublishing.com

Table of Contents

Dedication

This book is dedicated to every individual who has lost hope. We pray our story strengthens your FAITH and causes you to realize that there is NOTHING more powerful than trusting God and unconditional love! Faith and love don't just MOVE mountains, it puts us on TOP of them!

Introduction:
Faith & Love... A Divine Connection

My parents were married 50-plus years. I had a great example of marriage. They didn't even argue in front of me. Trent had a totally different example of what marriage should be. My parents built a business from the ground up. There were many sacrifices and lots of open affection. I marveled at their relationship growing up and I wanted to be married to a man just like my father.

In fact, when Trent and I met, marriage was the furthest thing from his mind. So, when it came to love and relationships Trent and I couldn't have been more opposite, but let Trent tell it...He keeps saying that's why we attract.

Alright folks, I must agree with my wife because I never thought my life would intersect with someone like her. It was like Rick Ross meets Michele Obama (where do they do that)? Irish is bougie and I am innately "hood," —and proud of it. However, eventually I understood that there were levels to this. Bougie, as far as I knew, included people who were arrogant, condescending, and more concerned with appearances and status. Irish wasn't, her bougieness was different; it was about her character and taste for the finer things in life. More importantly, she challenged me to be a better man and live a better life in all aspects; not just financially or materialistically. Irish caused me to question everything I knew about life, manhood, fatherhood, and especially love.

So, it is safe to say that Trent is attracted to my bougieness because it was my heart, drive, and kindness that drew him in and he cosigned on this divine adventure [that's been filled with unbelievable twists, a lot of turns and blessings in disguise] ... Our connection is one of them. I know our lives would be totally different if we hadn't divinely connected at "Exquisite Car Wash."

Chapter 1

Love ~~Angles~~ Angels

We met in 2004, while I was in pharmacy school. He was at his friend's car wash who happened to be the owner. Trent approached me with a smile, and he started talking to me as if we had known each other our entire lives. Our conversation escalated from typical introductions to plans for family barbecues and fishing trips. His conversational appeal intrigued me, and we continued our friendly chats sporadically for 10 years. Whenever he'd call, I was like hmmm; although, it felt as if I'd known him my entire life. We talked about almost everything and how we grew up. And even though we only talked twice a year, we'd pick right up where we left off…it was the oddest thing ever.; it had to be divine. The lenses in which we perceived love were different, we both experienced relationships from different angles.

Six months after meeting Trent, I was diagnosed with a brain tumor. I sat with the academic advisory board and the group of physicians all recommended that I withdraw from pharmacy school due to my declining health and inability to perform. Additionally, I didn't have the capacity to focus on a relationship with Trent because I was already in a stressful relationship.

Trent, on the other hand, had no clue what was happening in my life. I never disclosed the lows, just the highs, which in itself creates a false perception. Ironically, Trent always called when I needed to feel supported, secure, and ultimately comforted. This caused me to realize, there is nothing more divine than love. Trent's actions exuded love in the purest form, and I didn't even know it at the time.

Trent was married but he didn't confess it for several years. His actions proved he wasn't just trying to *hook up with me*. We never talked about *that*. I didn't find out he was married until the fourth year. Trent didn't tell me, God did. I was also in a toxic relationship, and I have never willingly walked into *drama*.

I adamantly stated, "You're married." He reluctantly admitted it, and it took around four years before he totally came clean. It was always something about him. God introduced us to each other while simultaneously preparing us *for* each other.

We started dating again in 2013, after Trent's divorce was final in 2012. He came to me and quite confidently said, "I want to date again." I responded, "You need time to heal…"

"Hold up, you told me if I got a divorce, we could get together." "No, I said you need to heal!" We never kissed, went on dates, or had any sexual encounters. Trent told me, telling him no (the boundaries and standards I put in place), is what made him pursue me even more; although, I knew he needed some inner-work.

To be honest, I was looking for love in all the wrong places, but I felt with Irish, I was finally looking in the right place. My life was in shambles and my broken inner child was driving my decisions and emotions, which is why my last marriage was on the rocks…The boy in me partly put it there. I wasn't ready for the responsibility of a lifelong commitment but was desperately ready to be *loved.* However, I've learned that you cannot love anyone until you learn to fully love yourself.

Prior to the divorce, in the last two years of my 13-year marriage, I cheated. As a result of my infidelity, I had a son. I was walking in my father's beat up shoes…ones I never knew I could wear but perfectly fit. I was my father's son—a rolling stone, and I have five children. I didn't know why I was wired the way I was, but since half of my DNA came from my father, who I never knew, it was inescapable. I was running from myself, but his shadow was always there. Like most young men, they aspire to be like their dad, but I had no clue…this wasn't a case of mistaken identity, but no identity at all. No, I'm not blaming my dad for stepping out on my first wife but being raised by a man who was supposed to be my father, and later finding out that he wasn't, caused a lot of voids in my life. Then I had a Michael Jackson moment, I had to face the man in the mirror. As I reflect, I had two prominent men in my life…my step dad who raised me, who divorced my mom when I was headed into high school. Then there was the man who signed my birth certificate; although, he knew I wasn't his son and vice versa. My biological father and mom wanted to keep me a secret. Then when I had my second youngest son, I tried to keep him a secret as well, but my conscience wouldn't let me. When I looked at him, I saw myself. It was time for me to man up because I knew what it felt like to be a secret.

So, when my son was a year old, I told my ex-wife. After I came clean, I left the same night. Honestly, I wanted and needed to leave…I wouldn't have slept well that night anyways because emotions were high. I felt extremely convicted because of my infidelity, but this was about personal accountability. This was a part of my healing process and stepping out of my daddy's ugly shoes. The upside to all of this… I was finally becoming an honest man, although I ended up homeless.

Thankfully, God, The Father never stopped *fathering* me, and I was finally at a point where I no longer denied that the issue was me! It amazes how God never outcasts us or deems us useless because of our faults. However, God uses the very things we despise about ourselves - to show the world how USEful it is! God's best work was always produced in the dirtiest places. And I was D-I-R-T-Y!

Divine Pursuit

Now that I look back on it, I realize my connection with Irish was divine. I am a spiritual person with flaws— and a lot of them. Ironically, Irish understood me better than most people. So, we continued to talk… no one had the ability to soothe me like her. God painted the picture "of us" perfectly!

She brushed me off a lot at first, which caused me to really pursue her. But Irish quickly reminded me that, "We are *not* exclusive." I didn't appreciate it either, so I stormed out of her place in my Timberlands. Not to mention, I had to climb three flights of stairs to get to her apartment.

She called me about three weeks later and I answered, although, I said I wasn't going to talk to her bossy and independent self any more. Irish asked, "Are you mad?" She didn't have to ask; she knew I was mad! I was ready to go steady and she just wasn't having it, but I continued my pursuit (heavily).

I kept pushing Trent away because I wasn't ready. I was afraid because I was *still* dealing with myself. I had finally achieved internal happiness. I was working, completing an internship, and improving my physical health. I was focused on me, God, and what was coming next...

Now Irish's view belonged to her, not me. I was looking for love and to be loved. I had attempted to fill the voids in my heart from the trauma of my rocky childhood, a rocky marriage, simply put a rocky life in general.

When I met Irish, it wasn't a come on. She was at the carwash. I felt like I was connected to her in some kind of way. I told Trent, "You feel like family." I came from a small town and honestly, I thought… Maybe he was my cousin, thankfully he wasn't!

In 2013, Trent proposed on Christmas Eve at Dorothy B. Oven Park, in front of everyone during the holiday night of lights. I was so embarrassed that I couldn't cry. I don't like attention or the forefront. In a matter-of-fact tone, I stated… "You could have asked me this at home and I would have said yes!"

We got engaged but we didn't marry until October 2014. Yes, we had some really good sex! Ironically, I wasn't worried about getting pregnant! During this time, Trent was putting together the pieces of his life… So, we went to Atlanta to visit his biological father, whom he met only once prior to this encounter. Upon our return, I couldn't shake the feeling of needing to take a pregnancy test… So, I did. It was positive.

We canceled our elaborate wedding plans and went to the courthouse. We felt God's divine love and that's all that mattered to us. The following Monday, we went to the bank to apply for a mortgage loan. Trent spent days and hours praying to God for an approval, although seven people placed bids on the fixer-upper. Even during the renovation process, Trent was very sick to the point of having to lay down on the floor for breaks.

Initially, it didn't hit me that it would be our home. Even during renovations, I would take brakes and lie on the floor. Irish would waddle in and help paint.

When we started dating, I saw a change in him. Trent became very active in the church. There was an aura about him. I said, "Whatever this is, I like this version of YOU." The changes I witnessed in Trent helped me let my guard down as I slowly allowed him to reveal himself to me.

As a man, I have a high-level of pride. Although, I told Irish most things; however, I chose not to tell her I was homeless, as a result of my divorce. I didn't want Irish's pity, her couch, or for her to think less of me.

Now as Trent pursued me, another well-known gentleman who was financially stable also attempted to court me. He provided fancy trips, unlimited shopping, and all the attention I wanted. However, there wasn't any chemistry between us… So, I let it go. I realized I needed more than material things to maintain my happiness—I needed a divine love connection. Because when the money's gone, divine love holds everything together and this is priceless.

Matters of the Heart

Before we were married, Trent told me that his family's medical history included heart issues. I was really hard on him, because I didn't understand heart failure or the gravity of his health issues.

I remember when he couldn't remember my name due to a stroke he had. He kept calling me "ma" and I was adamant about Trent calling me by my name. I told him plain and simple, "Don't call me if you can't remember my name…Would you want your daughter to date a man who couldn't remember her name?" I hung up the phone, although he repeatedly called me. I didn't answer until the next day. I answered the phone, and he called me by my name, Irish… He finally broke down and told me about his stroke that resulted in sporadic memory loss. I felt absolutely horrible!

Six months into our marriage, Trent's health issues hit us hard. The moment we had Caleb, Trent had countless doctor appointments. In fact, there were about twenty-seven hospital stays in one year. We were making $30K annually, which disqualified us for subsidized health insurance. If it were not for my mom and Trent's aunt, we wouldn't have made it. One year, we spent all of our birthdays, including major holidays, in the hospital. This was right before my heart transplant.

Trent's health challenges drastically affected our lives. The first six years of Caleb's life, we were constantly in and out of the hospital and as a result, our son struggled with social and emotional development. Trent even takes the blame for this… However, as Caleb's father, Trent constantly reminds him that he is strong, brave, and brilliant. Every day, Trent and Caleb do their signature handshake and they dap it up three times (one for the Father, the Son, and the Holy Ghost), then they look up towards heaven. This is what I fell in love with, a man after God's heart who would divinely heal him in every way.

Chapter 2

Love Doesn't Pay Bills

I attended church faithfully; it was like my second home. After services, I'd visit Irish. One night she said, "I really see a change in you." I was struggling with substance abuse, homelessness, relational trauma, and I was trying to find myself as a person. And at the age of forty-four, the weight of not knowing who my biological father was, was a secret I no longer wanted to carry. I had no clue Irish noticed my efforts to become a better man and her words validated me…at least I knew I was on the right path. It's hard putting pieces of your life together while toiling with triggers and traumas, but I was determined to discover a better version of myself.

I was at a breaking point. My mom was in rehab, and it felt as if the universe was on my shoulders. I was walking around with a lump in my throat. I needed loving assurance that things would work out. I asked Irish if I could come over and shower. She said yes… I felt everything was falling apart. We sat there and talked. I was transparent about my life and how I was transitioning. Irish never turned her nose up at me or passed judgment and I needed that.

At that moment, I felt even more connected to her. Our feelings were mutual, and we became inseparable. I had a cleaning business, and I was receiving disability. Irish wanted to start her own business. I told her, Man… I've listened to a lot of motivational speakers. Steve Harvey, one of my all-time favorites, came on TV, and said, "you want to start a business, just jump." I told her. "Baby God is showing us the signs—Let's jump! Irish, (who counts every dime and predicts every storm) said, "but Trent, we don't have nothing." I responded, "Exactly, so all we have to do is trust God."

*Trust in the LORD with all your heart and **lean not** on **your own understanding**; in all your ways submit to him, and he will make your paths straight.*
(Proverbs 3:5-6 NIV)

The Testing

We were so broke, that to this day, most of our clients are as broke as we were (divine relativity). God set it up just like that, so we'd be empathetic. Rally's had four for four and that was considered a treat for the up-and-coming founders and CEOs of Avail Health and Behavioral Solutions & Avail Transport Services.

I wanted to start this business, but Trent was reluctant in the beginning. We started our business in April 2016, we depleted our savings and used our tax return as seed money for startup. My mom passed away in January 2016 of a stroke and heart failure; Caleb was eight- months-old. At that point, I hit the ground running. My mom and Trent's aunt, Mary Porter, supported us financially. Without them, we wouldn't have made it. Not only was my mom's death a passing of a torch, but the baton. I could hear her say, "stick, you got this baby girl."! My mom left me in charge of everything. That stress and burden fell on me and Trent.

Soon after, we experienced some turmoil within our family, finances, our careers, and personal life. I felt as if we had nothing else left to lose…I lost my mom and I was about to be terminated from my place of employment, I was devastated! However, Trent told me to jump! So, I put in my two-week notice, to focus on my entrepreneurial goals.

The same day I resigned; I received an email from my first client. He solidified an $11K contract with our company. My entire being immediately "woosah'ed," Trent looked at me and said, "Let's go to the movies!" And we did. God showed us again that we (me and Trent) are meant to be together. Apart from each other we were okay, but together we are divine!

Two months after we launched our business, Trent's health took another turn for the worse! At the time, Trent's medical conditions included diabetes, hypertension, mental issues, and congestive heart failure.

I felt terrible, my body retained so much fluid, I was rushed to the ER weekly in Tallahassee.

Unfortunately, during my last visit there, the ER Physician nonchalantly said, "We will drain the as much fluid as we can, but there is nothing else we can do." She basically sent me home to die, and to add injury to insult the doctor was a Black woman. I know that she didn't owe me anything, but I expected her to at least act like she cared.

Chapter 3

Faith & Love

After this incident with Dr. I Don't Care, both Irish and I experienced a sense of hopelessness we had never experienced before. My health took a toll on our marriage, our business, family life, and our own personal issues. Our baby was two years old and *still* not talking. Although we knew Caleb's speech impediment was not our fault, naturally we blamed ourselves. We also did everything we could to help him… We sought out the best speech therapist, occupational therapist, and every educational resource available.

During this time Trent's health continued to decline, his heart was functioning at only seven percent. I thought I was going to lose Trent, but my love for him wouldn't allow me to give up hope. I did everything the doctors instructed me to do for Trent while we waited for his L-VAC approval. However, everything overwhelmed me! My faith wasn't just being tested in every way and it was difficult to keep going.

Trent and I maintained our love through it all, we never grew tired of each other. It was our love that strengthened us. Our focus was ensuring that Trent received the best care possible. Surprisingly, Trent's faith never wavered although he was literally walking through a *valley of death*. He encouraged me to keep believing because of his faith… In his words, "I have BIG faith, so should you!"

Our relationship was built on faith and love, and as we realized that our actions had to prove daily that we were committed to each other. We experienced the worst before we experienced better… What is worse than death? We had MORE living to do, and I understood that my purpose here on earth had not been *completely* fulfilled yet. For this reason alone, I believe my faith wouldn't let me die! If I had died, too much would've died with me.

Our lives epitomized our vows, "to have and to hold from this day forward, for better, for worse, for richer, for poorer, in sickness and in health, to love and to cherish, until parted by death." Our union was strengthened and solidified on faith and love; our faith convinced us that our love was strong enough to endure any and everything we would experience. Thankfully, God has allowed our hearts to go on…

19

Chapter 4

Heart Maintenance

Getting in the Trenches

I received the first L-VAC in 2017. My heart was literally broken; although I felt hopeless, I never felt it was my time to leave here. The L-VAC procedure was fairly new and expensive. Initially, I was denied medical coverage on all fronts—for the devices and a heart transplant. We were told I didn't "meet the qualifications". At the time, I only had subsidized health insurance. Nevertheless, God sent an advocate in the form of a doctor who strategically guided us through the process of getting approved.

The journey to living wasn't without discipline. However, I wanted to live, I was determined to live so I committed to changes. My A1C levels typically lingered around thirteen and my glucose level consistently stayed around 800. None of these numbers were normal and I went about my daily activities as if nothing was wrong. I didn't want to allow the way I felt to keep me from "being a man."

I was extremely sick — because I was dying! And if I didn't commit to bettering my health, I would have left here prematurely. Nevertheless, Irish was there with me every step of the way! She learned everything she needed to know about my health conditions (diabetes, hypertension, congestive heart failure, high cholesterol, and prostate issues). Although she went to school to become a healthcare administrator, she was my personal healthcare advocate.

We took heed to the instructions of my doctor, and I worked to improve my overall health. This was the only way I could get approved for my first L-VAC. I was on a low-sodium, low-carb, low-fat diet (N-A-S-T-Y!). I didn't drink or smoke. The one time I had a drink, it showed up in my labs and that set us back. I had to be 100 percent clean, sober, and pure…no ifs ands or buts about it.

This was a physical, mental, and spiritual journey that presented countless obstacles. I struggled because my illnesses were debilitating beyond my control. I learned to be vulnerable and "manning up meant" laying down…I had to surrender. Just walking a few paces was exhausting. Bills were coming in and Caleb was still an energetic toddler. Irish and I were trying to figure out how to run our business, raise our son, and hold on to our marriage. I was calling shots from my sick bed …whether in my bed at home or at Shands Hospital in Gainesville, FL.

Scared to Death

In December 2017, while hospitalized, I received the news that my L-VAC procedure was approved a few days before Christmas—the BEST gift ever, although it took 12 hours. I was on mandatory life support for 72 hours. Everything worked, and my numbers looked great according to the doctors. Besides Jesus, I was the other Christmas miracle, my FAITH remains BIG!

Three weeks later, I was released to a hotel in Gainesville to ensure that Irish could properly take care of me. The level of care we received was amazing but overwhelming. Caleb was in the capable hands of Aunt Mary, which allowed us to focus on my recovery. Eventually, we returned to our home in Tallahassee. I still had wires and machines connected to me.

We couldn't afford a power failure. Irish contacted the city to ensure we maintained power. The batteries for the L-VAC had to be changed every eight- to 10 hours. Not to mention, we had to have backup batteries. One too many times, we forgot the battery pack and we only had minutes to ensure Trent would live.

We had a death scare in 2018, during hurricane season. Irish and I left Tallahassee, and we took shelter at a resort in Orlando. I took my son down to the pool while Irish worked on some billing. When we got to the pool, Caleb asked to get on the slide. As I watched my son come down, I saw him go underwater but he did not come back up. Without hesitation, I jumped in the pool to save him. My L-VAC could NOT get wet… I nearly committed suicide saving my son!

Once my son was safe, I realized my L-VAC was beeping - it sounded like I was flat-lining. I called Irish and said, "I'm 'bout to go! My machine is making a flat-line sound. I love you, bye." I hung up the phone and the EMT got me to Orlando Regional Medical Center in the knick of time. If we had arrived one milliliter of a second later, I would be dead—But GOD said, "It's not your time!"

I was immediately taken to triage; the batteries were replaced (in two seconds) and I was released in under an hour. I was fine. Irish could have done the same procedure, but everything was left at home in Tallahassee. This was another sign that God's hand was on my life! I wasn't ready to go, and God didn't take me, although Irish was ready to lay hands on me for scaring her to death. To Irish's surprise, I was sitting in the waiting room chilling (with my feet crossed and all) when she arrived.

We returned to the resort because the power was still out in Tallahassee. We made the most of our time in Central Florida and visited Disney World and Animal Kingdom. However, this wasn't enough to undo the trauma Caleb endured from the near-drowning incident. In fact, he is still terrified of water (pools in particular), and we've taken him to therapy. I pray one day he'll swim like a fish, but until then, we'll steer clear of pools.

A setback

About eight months after we returned home and got adjusted to the L-VAC, out of the blue, our life spiraled *again*. Trent developed a blood clot, which is the number one cause of death in L-VAC patients. Trent started retaining fluid and had to be airlifted to the hospital in Gainesville. I got on the road. They performed emergency surgery… opened Trent up and replaced the entire L-VAC. It was the same routine as the first procedure. He had to be on life support for 72 hours.

God sent another angel in the form of a fellow patient who also had the same procedure and she encouraged us. She's had her L-VAC for years. Nevertheless, Trent's surgery went well. He just wasn't responding to the recovery. His numbers did not look good at all.

The family was coming in and out of the hospital because everyone thought Trent was about to die. I had to get control of the situation, so I decided that no one else would come see Trent because I believe this was causing his numbers to go up. I stayed in the room with him for seven days…Me, God, and gospel music. I built an altar in a corner near a window around the machines. I even reached out to gospel recording artist Trey Mclaughlin and The Sounds of Zamar. He even wrote me back. Although I felt numb and broken, I displayed my faith through worship. My prayer was a plea for God to spare Trent. We needed a miracle and that's what I anticipated - It was in this moment I developed BIG FAITH!

Things started to shift. The doctor said they were going to add an R-VAC, this was on a Sunday, and I signed all of the paperwork for Trent to undergo surgery. I prayed like crazy in the midst of the chaos and finally rested. I woke up Monday morning at 6 a.m. to a doctor stating that he turned off the machines and Trent was breathing on his own. Praise JESUS! This reminds me of the story when Jesus was in the boat and there was a storm, but Jesus rested. Thirty minutes later, Trent looked over at me. I was overwhelmed with gratitude and appreciation for God's grace and mercy.

Thankfully, God gave us the strength to stand, and Trent received another miracle! The greatest lesson from this experience was to trust God, even when it looks like the odds were clearly stacked against us.

Chapter 5

Love Has NO Secrets

My momma always said, "When you get married and have your own man… You will understand, just keep living and learning." I didn't understand the gravity of my mom's words of wisdom until Trent and I got together. Our backgrounds are vastly different, and it shaped the way we perceive everything - especially our relationship.

My parents were married for 56-years, and their relationship is a testament of true commitment. Up until I was 15 years old, my father could do no wrong… Unfortunately, this all changed when I recognized the smell of my father's cologne coming from another girl at my high school…

My friends and I were standing around talking, when another female student passed by waving her money. It wasn't the flashing of her money that snatched my attention, it was the smell of my father's cologne coming from the money. You see, my dad always sprayed his money with three different colognes. The smell was unmistakable, I could recognize it anywhere!

So, I walked up to her and asked, "Where did you get that money from?" She looked at me and mockingly said, "*Our* daddy gave it to me!" I didn't exchange any more words; my fist met her face, and she met the ground! Then I jumped on top of her and started fighting her again. I could hear my friends saying, "Beat that a** Irish, and I did. As expected, I got suspended for five days and I had too much time to ponder the girl's accusation.

I needed answers, but my parents never provided an explanation because the girl's statement was true. I was a child and I had to stay in a child's place. My parents' marital issues were theirs and not mine. However, I was still drastically affected by it. My dad was taking care of another woman and her kids, and my mom stayed and cared for him as if He never did anything wrong. I judged my mother because I didn't understand her loyalty and love for *her husband* - but I fully understand it now! Love doesn't have secrets.

Secret Conception Has No Love

I've always had a keen sense of discernment before I knew what it was. At the age of fifteen, my mother almost wrecked her blue Toyota station wagon when I said this, "Ma, I have something to ask you." "Yes, Trent." She firmly stated, and I proceeded to talk. "The man you claimed is my father, is not my dad!" Momma raised her voice and said, "Who told you that!" I responded, "The holy spirit, He told me to ask you!" My mom didn't believe me, but she couldn't deny the truth either.

From that day forward, emptiness and loneliness consumed me. The trust I had in my mother was crushed and I carried this distrust into every relationship I had (until I met Irish). Now, I was searching for love and someone to love me *truthfully* but how could I find what I didn't recognize. I confused sex with love at an early age, and at age 16, I became a father. I was still living with my mom, and she forbade me from seeing my child and her mother. I had to secretly spend time with my daughter because I feared being abandoned and homeless.

I felt heartbroken every time I left my baby girl, Jessica. I couldn't understand why my mom wanted me to be an absent father. Although I had an open invitation to move in with my daughter and her mom, I couldn't leave *my* mom even though our relationship had no trust. My mom had secrets, and she wanted me to repeat her cycle of detrimental hidden truths, but love shouldn't have secrets. Then again, maybe secrets are designed to protect the real truth and always someone's reputation or "good name."

So, I continued to wander through my teen years with no real sense of who I was and who I was to be to my daughter. The fact that I was a father of a precious baby girl who also looked like me was crazy. I secretly prayed she would turn out alright because I knew even then I wasn't equipped to nurture, provide, or love her the way she needed but I did the best I could.

The love I experienced and gave had several secrets. After becoming a teenage father, I realized that I needed the love that I attempted to give. I felt numb, my mother (of all people) had deceived me, and I felt she didn't deserve my trust. However, I protected her and never told her secrets, but no one protected me - especially from myself. I smoked plenty of weed to cope with life and I sold a few bags to cover pampers, wipes and baby food. I also gave my baby momma some money to keep her mouth shut because I didn't want her to write me off as deadbeat dad.

My early adult years consisted of attempting to find love and making babies. In fact, I impregnated two women pregnant within one year. I was twenty-two with three kids, unmarried and wasn't ready to commit to anyone, not even myself. All of this happened four years after my first daughter was born…my life was heavy but not heavy enough to take my own life (ever).

The drama was always too much to deal with! I was dating two women, and I was *feeling* one more than the other. When my second baby momma told me she was pregnant a light went off. I knew it wasn't good to keep contributing to the human race lackadaisically and besides, kids were expensive. I cut ties with Cameron's mom and chose Jalen's mother. This created more DRAMA! This situation drove me crazy because I just wanted to be a father. Seemingly, calm co-parenting wasn't an option at all.

Then I saw things as they were. I wasn't trying to hear the noise and channeled my energy towards the moms who would just let me at least see my kids. I did my best to hold down a job and show up on more than birthdays. Sometimes that meant testing the water by calling first to check on their attitude. Seems like they'd go from zero to one hundred when they saw my phone number pop up.

I am still working on having relationships with all my kids and their moms [and I mean I'm working hard]. Some relationships are easier than others, but I've learned to do my best and let God do the rest. We finally made it to a calm space of co-parenting but having a toxic sexual *situationship* disrupted that peace quickly!

The beginning of our end was near… One day my bm called me and I ended the call abruptly. She said she was just calling to check on me. Her actions seemed suspicious, and I blew a fuse. I headed to her house immediately and I was packing heat. When I arrived, I knocked on the door and she refused to answer! There was NO DAMN way I was going to stand outside. So, I broke the window and let myself in…

BM was crying hysterically and yelling for me not to hurt her sneaky link. I wasn't hearing any of that sh**. I told Mr. Sneaky link to sit his punk-ass down, and he sat down immediately. No questions asked! In the meantime, I was unaware that my BM called the police. Then I heard Jalen crying, and I snapped out of my rage momentarily. So, I went to the bedroom, picked up my son and put my gun back in my car. As I attempted to leave with my son, I was met by police officers and placed under arrest. A female officer carefully de-escalated our volatile domestic dispute and after about 20 minutes, she took my son away from me and I was taken to jail.

The charges were stacked against me…from burglary of a dwelling to felony battery. But I didn't even touch anyone; just a bunch of trumped-up charges. Now I admit that I broke a window to get into the house, but everything else needed to be dropped. Nevertheless, that situation was a lesson learned, which was to never allow my emotions to carry me to a place where I have no self-control.

I was consumed with anger and rage while I was locked up. I told God, "I swear I am gonna kill all of them MFs. I ain't did sh**, EVERYBODY GOTTA DIE!" On this night, I wrestled with myself and God ALL night! My heavenly father wouldn't allow my thoughts to manifest as a reality. God saw the BEST in me, although, I was doing everything I could to bring out the worst in me.

Thankfully, murder wasn't the case that was given to me… and I vowed to be a better father and person over all… but my coping mechanisms only masked my pain. After years of drinking, smoking, selling, and using drugs I had another life-changing epiphany. I needed more and I believed marriage was the answer.

Although, I prayed about marriage… I never asked God to guide me. My decision was based on my emotions, and if I haven't learned anything - I know my heart is deceitful. I tricked myself into my first marriage… I wasn't ready in any way shape or form. I married into a blended family, something I never wanted!

I stayed in my first marriage for approximately thirteen years. The last five years of my marriage were almost unbearable. At the time, my ex-wife was holy-rolling. I wasn't with it, I was for the streets, for real!

Chapter 6

Child #4… Devin's Conception

I know my relationSHIT was careless, funky, and messy! Most of the conflicts in my life during this time were because I initiated them in some type of way.

While I was coaching a celebrity football camp (for boys 9-12) when I met baby momma four. Her oldest son was enrolled. I casually introduced myself and we started talking. During our conversations, we found out that she knew my best friend, Brent. A couple weeks later Brent called and told me she wanted my phone number, which led to a lot of booty calls. I never denied being married, and she didn't care and neither did I, obviously.

Six months into my infidelity, Devin was conceived. I was like dang! I wasn't ready for none of that —fatherhood or drama AGAIN, but I'd never turn my back on my own flesh and blood. So, I manned up AFTER a year and disclosed Devin to my wife. The secret was haunting me. It was like I was waking up every day to keep the secret from her. I was living my own life over again…this was the exact same thing my mom and dad did to me. I was haunted by my own reality!

When I admitted I had f*cked up *again*, my ex-wife still wanted to work things out. Although she was angry, she was still more understanding than I expected. However, I was done because I was already checked out of our marriage. I didn't want to try anymore and even though I didn't have a place to go, I figured sleeping in my car would give me more peace. So, I left… technically, I was homeless and starting over *again* at the age of 41.

I knew my life needed direction, because my choices weren't taking me where I wanted to go. Like most of us, I turned to God and the church. I started attending church more regularly, but I felt judged and talked about because my ex-wife told several people about our issues. I spoke with my pastor, and he advised me to keep coming to church, and I did. I started serving and became very involved in church.

In addition to seeking God, I also sought therapy (just like my pastor). I knew my life was in shambles because of the decisions I made, not anyone else. My distrust in people made it very difficult (initially)for me to discuss my problems with my pastor/counselor. However, because he kept it real with me, I was able to be honest with myself, God, and him. His life is an open book and so is mine, now. People can't hold things against you once you're free indeed. Not even the chatter or gossip can hold you back.

About a year later, my divorce was finalized, and my healing journey continued. I thought Irish would be ready to move forward, but this heffa told me that I wasn't healed, and I had more self-work to do. Admittedly, [to myself], I did because when she would try to hold me accountable, I'd run back to one of my baby mommas (until the toxic cycle got really old). See, when I came clean with God, it required a thorough cleansing mentally, physically, and spiritually [Isaiah 26:3 NIV]. Now, I understand that my deliverance and healing is a continual process of self-evaluation and accountability; for this, I am grateful.

Chapter 7

Demolishing Generational Cycles

As the *New* Porters… what was, will be no more. This isn't only a prayer, but a joint, intentional decision not only to be better but to do better…because we *know* better!

When I decided I wouldn't hide my son like I was hidden, I knew things would be different for me. I had three dads (four with God). One raised me (Bobby), one moved away and I kept a relationship with him (I'm named after him); although he *isn't* my real dad (Enell). I also stayed with him off -and-on as a troubled kid. Then there was my biological father (Sam). I finally met him in July 2013 at a family reunion. I was about forty-five at the time. It was a surreal moment because I was getting my life together and things were falling into place. Not knowing who I was had haunted me all of my life. This was a key part of breaking the cycle. In fact, that weekend, my wife, and I conceived our son, Caleb…I was FREE.

I told my dad that I didn't want anything from him but needed a blood test and would pay for it prior to us connecting. I just wanted to confirm who I was. I reached out to my dad's sister, Janice, first. She organized the blood test. Aunt Janice played a major role in my journey of piecing my life together.

Looking back, I realized that I had a lot of men in my life, but I always felt alone. Maybe because there was no real connection. I had male figures but was so broken, I couldn't see the value in them. Nevertheless, my relationship with my biological father is alright, and I am still going through therapy. My dad was selfish and abandoned me and my siblings. I still have moments of unrest, but I know how to check-in with myself.

Despite the fragmented relationship with my father, I realized our family needed a strong patriarchal presence. I was ready to accept this mantle and with my wife, Irish, it was much easier than I anticipated. Her support, advice, encouragement, and innate motherly nature helped everything run smoothly.

In fact, in 2021, we planned a family trip to California at the suggestion of a relative. I told him to talk to his wife and he said, "she'd love to go out there to see her daddy." Irish planned the whole trip in one day. It was just what I needed! Dad and I organized the Thanksgiving meal. The food was awful! It was a Mexican soul food restaurant that prepared the food. Dad recommended the restaurant because he lived in LA, but I trusted him and rolled with it.

Best of all, were the memories with family on a major holiday. Since that time, we communicate more frequently and see each other more often. We even do day trips. We are now making the most of everything as we continue to build our relationships.

My greatest lesson in all of this is knowing it's never too late to step in as a healed father, son, brother, nephew and most importantly, husband. So, I extended my biological father the *same* grace that God granted me. This is how we crush the generational cycles!

Chapter 8

In Sickness & Health

We've had countless health crises. The tests we've faced were at the onset of our union, but they prepared us for where we are now. Back in November 2019, the hospital became our home *again*. Thankfully, we knew what to do—hunker down, believe, and weather another storm.

However, this time, I needed two transplants for my heart and kidney because my heart wasn't beating at full capacity and my other organs were distressed. I spent all of our birthdays in a hospital bed. What was even more disappointing was the cancellation of my birthday trip to LA.

After three months of being hospitalized, I moved from the bottom of the donor waiting list to the first recipient in only 2 months! This was a miraculous moment in my life! My doctors rejected two hearts while I was waiting because they weren't strong enough. The organ donor that saved my life was a healthy 19-year-old male. I received my heart transplant on February 28, 2020, at 12 a.m. and I received my kidney transplant 12 hours later.

When they told me they had a heart, the doctor and his team of physicians came to me. I was transferred to the children's unit. I was there with pediatric heart patients and a nurse. This was the nurse's first time in this unit, and I could hear some commotion in the background. She came in crying hysterically and I eventually learned a child had passed away. I was full of tears. I asked "God, why are you keeping me here, and taking these children?! I'm filthy like a dirty rag and there's no reason that I can see to still be here. From that point on, I knew God had a plan and a purpose…most importantly, He is sovereign. Then I heard, "I have you here for My purpose."

The Transplant Transition

In March of 2020, I had to call the paramedics to the transition house, Trent's oxygen levels were extremely low. When I arrived at the hospital, I was placed on life support to save my organs - I had contracted COVID-19 (my entire family tested positive).

Again, I didn't feel like I was going to die. I called Irish on facetime and promised her, "I'm not going to leave you and I mean it." However, because of the global pandemic, she couldn't come into the hospital, everything was locked down. It was just me and Jesus! God showed up as *usual*... Second chances are a cliche, God has given me too many. Two months passed before we were able to go home. I had to be tested every three days and be free of COVID before I was released. Irish and I snuck home on two different occasions because we simply MISSED being at our home. So many things could have happened, but God watched over us.

After this experience, I was featured on a CNN Father's Day Special. God put my life on display for His glory, and I was overwhelmed with gratitude! Not from the seeming instant popularity or fame, but I was consumed with thankfulness because of God's grace, mercy, provision, plans, and purpose for my life! As soon as I was able to walk, I hit the ground running and serving!

Through the outreach programs at my church, I worked with Farm Share and Daily Bread Ministries for nearly a whole year. These organizations provide free food to the community at large for those in need. I was excited to serve because I knew I shouldn't have been alive, but God saw otherwise!

While I was serving, I was supposed to be recording a live television interview. Irish called me in straight manager mode, "Where the hell you at? These people are calling me asking for you - YOU are making us look bad!" I responded in my best King Jaffe's voice, "They can wait, I'm about my Father's business 'ret' NOW… Let 'em wait!" Needless to say, Irish didn't share my feelings. According to her, my actions were unprofessional, but they were purposeful. The news outlet's plans were NOT bigger or more important than God's plans for *my* life.

The next day, we conducted the interview… they waited. Our story inspired so many people to give to us randomly, but we didn't accept it. However, we intentionally sowed into others because we were extremely blessed, and we had more than enough to share. Although most people were grateful, we still experienced betrayal from those who were self-serving and self-seeking. We (Me and Irish) completely understood that our true source was God and each other. We stood firm on God's promises, and He has continued to bless us!

Chapter 9

Good Things *Can* Last Forever

The love Trent and I share is far from cliche! We never lived in a fairytale, but clutches of real-life experiences that produced *real* love. We understood, almost immediately, that love in action always TRUMPED simply saying "I love you!" God divinely orchestrated our love, and because of that we cherish each other wholeheartedly. Both of our lives changed for the better when God connected us - our love was never a one-way street, but a highway created just for us.

My mantra as it relates to marriage, has always been "one and done!" I meant that… because marriage is supposed to last forever! It is a good thing - better yet the BEST thing. Trent and I haven't allowed anything to be an asunder in our lives… health, past relationships, family issues, finances— nothing has separated us from our love for each other or God.

Irish is THE BEST I've ever had… My baby ain't just good - SHE IS GOD GOOD (it's a difference)! She is my blessing on top of my blessings! She makes everything better and sweeter. How sweet it is to be loved by HER!

After my divorce, I believed that I would never marry *again*… then God connected our paths. Even though we were on the same path, I was still the one pursuing her. My gut told me - she was my "good thing." And I believed it until it happened… So here we are. This is us - Irish and Trent—The new Porters… Our love connection is divine because we've stood on BIG FAITH! This love is BEYOND us!

About the Authors

Irish and Trent Porter's journey began over 21 years ago in the most unexpected of places—a car wash near the Florida A&M University campus on a serene evening. Little did they know that this chance encounter would set the stage for a remarkable life together.

Irish, hailing from the charming small town of Lake Placid, FL, was immersed in her studies at Florida A&M University, diligently working towards completing a final exam. Meanwhile, Trent, a Tallahassee native, found himself at the same car wash, unaware that destiny was about to unfold.

Over the next decade, Irish and Trent maintained a connection that transcended the ordinary. They communicated, sharing life updates and experiences, all the while blissfully unaware of the divine plan that was unfolding in the background.

In 2016, their shared dreams took shape as they co-founded a community-based healthcare company, driven by their passion for making a positive impact on the well-being of others. The following year marked a new chapter in their entrepreneurial journey as they ventured into the trucking industry, establishing a second successful business in 2020.

As their professional lives flourished, so did their personal ones. In March 2015, Irish and Trent welcomed their miracle child, Caleb, into the world. Caleb, a true blessing, became the joyous center of their lives, solidifying the bond that began over two decades ago.

Looking back, Irish and Trent now understand that their paths were intricately woven together by a higher force. The car wash meeting, once seemingly ordinary, was the inception of a love story that would unfold with divine precision. Today, Irish and Trent are not only life partners but also successful business collaborators, sharing their lives with their beloved son, a loyal dog, and the flourishing ventures they built together. Their story is a testament to the magic that can unfold when two hearts, unbeknownst to them at first, are destined to beat as one.

www.ingramcontent.com/pod-product-compliance
Lightning Source LLC
Chambersburg PA
CBHW040135150726
48005CB00015B/2515